Black Widow Spider

Monica Harris

Heinemann Library
Chicago, Illinois

Customer Service 888-454-2279
Visit our website at www.heinemannlibrary.com

Designed by Ginkgo Creative, Inc.
Printed and bound in the United States by Lake Book Manufacturing, Inc.
Photo research by Scott Braut

07 06 05 04 03
10 9 8 7 6 5 4 3 2 1

Library of Congress Cataloging-in-Publication Data
Harris, Monica, 1964-
   Black widow spider / Monica Harris.
      p. cm. — (Bug books)
Summary: An introduction to the physical characteristics, habits, and natural environment of the black widow, one of the world's most poisonous spiders.
Includes bibliographical references (p.   ).
   ISBN: 1-40340-762-2 (HC), 1-40340-992-7 (Pbk.)
   1. Black widow spider—Juvenile literature. [1. Black widow spider. 2. Spiders.] I. Title. II. Series.
   QL458.42.T54 H37 2003
   595.4'4—dc21

                    2002004014

Acknowledgments
The author and publishers are grateful to the following for permission to reproduce copyright material:
pp. 4, 7 Dr. James L. Castner; p. 5 E. R. Degginger/Photo Researchers, Inc.; pp. 6, 16, 23 James C. Cokendolpher; p. 8 Tom McHugh/Photo Researchers, Inc.; pp. 9, 12 J. H. Robinson/Photo Researchers, Inc.; p. 10 Ann & Rob Simpson; p. 11 David T. Roberts/Nature's Images/Photo Researchers, Inc.; pp. 13, 14, 15, 24 Daniel Heuclin/NHPA; p. 17 Mark Cassino; p. 18 Robert Brenner/PhotoEdit; p. 19 Index Stock Imagery, Inc.; p. 20 Dane S. Johnson/Visuals Unlimited; pp. 21, 25, 28 James H. Robinson; p. 22 Museum of Science Boston; p. 26 David A. Northcott/Corbis; p. 27 Visuals Unlimited; p. 29 Doug Sokell/Visuals Unlimited.

Illustration, p. 30, by Will Hobbs.
Cover photograph by Scott Camazine/Oxford Scientific Films.

Every effort has been made to contact copyright holders of any material reproduced in this book. Any omissions will be rectified in subsequent printings if notice is given to the publisher.

Special thanks to Dr. William Shear, Department of Biology, Hampden-Sydney College, for his review of this book.

Some words are shown in bold, **like this**. You can find out what they mean by looking in the glossary.

Contents

What Are Black Widow Spiders?

Black widow **spiders** are **arachnids.**
They have eight legs and eight eyes.
Black widows can be brown or black.

Black widows make **silk webs** to
trap **insects.** Then they use special
mouthparts to kill them. Black
widow spiders are very **venomous.**

What Do Black Widow Spiders Look Like?

The black widow's body has two parts. The head and chest are in the smaller part. This part is called the **cephalothorax.** The larger part is the **abdomen.**

Black widows have red marks under their abdomens. The marks can be two small dots or two triangles connected at their points. **Males** also have red stripes on their sides.

How Big Are Black Widow Spiders?

The black widow's body is about the size of a pea. Its two front legs are longer than its other legs.

The **male** has a much smaller body and longer legs than the **female.** His **abdomen** is shaped like an egg. The female's abdomen is round.

How Are Black Widow Spiders Born?

Black widow **spiders mate** in the spring. Then the **female** makes a **silk egg sac.** The silk comes from her **spinnerets.** She lays from 250 to 750 eggs inside the egg sac.

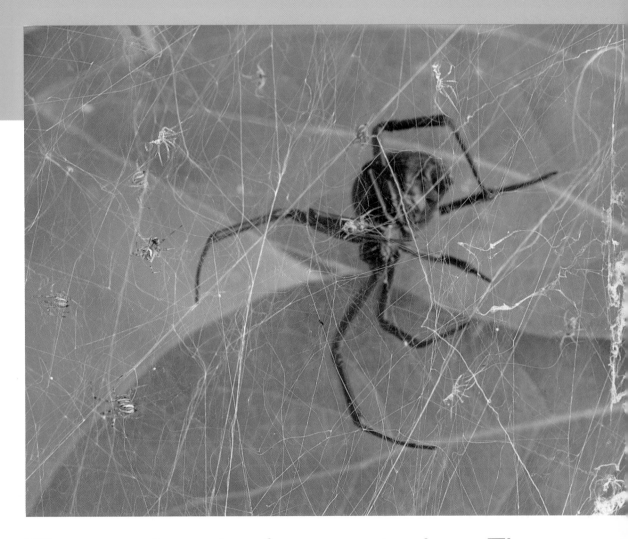

The eggs **hatch** after twenty days. The baby spiders are called **spiderlings.** They are tiny and white. Spiderlings stay in the **web** with their mother, but she doesn't take care of them.

How Do Black Widow Spiders Grow?

As **spiderlings** grow, their skin becomes too small. They shed their skin for a bigger one. This is called **molting.**

When the spiderlings are old enough, they spin a thread of **silk.** The wind catches the thread. The spiderling floats away to a new home. It moves like a balloon in the wind.

What Do Black Widow Spiders Eat?

Black widow **spiders** eat **insects** like crickets and cockroaches. They make a **web** of sticky **silk.** Insects get stuck in the web.

They use **fangs** to put **venom** into insects. The venom stops the **prey** from moving. Then, the spiders suck the juices from the insect's body.

Which Animals Attack Black Widow Spiders?

Wasps and other **spiders,** like this pirate spider, eat black widows. Black widows try to run away. Sometimes they lift their front legs in the air to scare the **predator** away.

This wasp will sting a black widow spider and put it into a nest with her eggs. The wasp **larvae** will eat the spider when they **hatch.**

Where Do Black Widow Spiders Live?

Black widows live in warm places. They build their **webs** away from people. A black widow **spider** might make a home in a pile of wood.

Black widows also live in storage sheds, outdoor toilets, trash piles, or hollow trees. **Females** live in dark places. They move around at night.

How Long Do Black Widow Spiders Live?

Female black widows live longer than **males.** They usually live about eighteen months. Males live about seven months.

Some baby black widows live for only a few days. **Spiderlings** are very hungry when they **hatch.** Sometimes they eat each other. This is called **cannibalism.**

How Do Black Widow Spiders Move?

claws

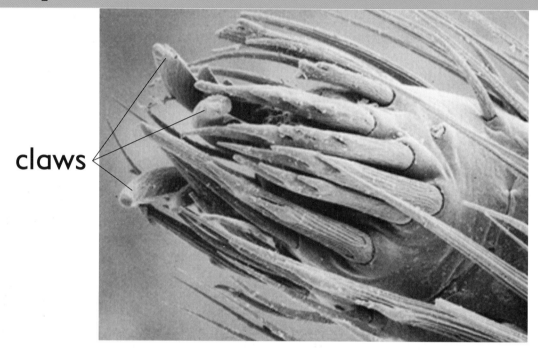

Spiders use their eight legs to walk. Three small claws at the end of each leg help them to hang onto things. They can even walk up walls.

Females hang upside down in their **webs.** They only leave when in danger. **Males** do not spin webs. When they leave their burrow, they walk on the ground to find food.

What Do Black Widow Spiders Do?

The **female** black widow may eat the **male** after they **mate.** But they usually just eat lots of **insects.** This **protects** gardens because insects eat lots of plants.

Each female makes from four to nine **egg sacs** in the summer. There are thousands of eggs. But only a few **spiderlings** will live to become **adults.**

How Are Black Widow Spiders Special?

The black widow is one of the most **venomous spiders.** But only **females** have **venom.** One drop is more deadly than a drop of rattlesnake venom!

These spiders are very shy. They usually do not bite humans. Most bites happen when people run into a black widow's **web** by mistake.

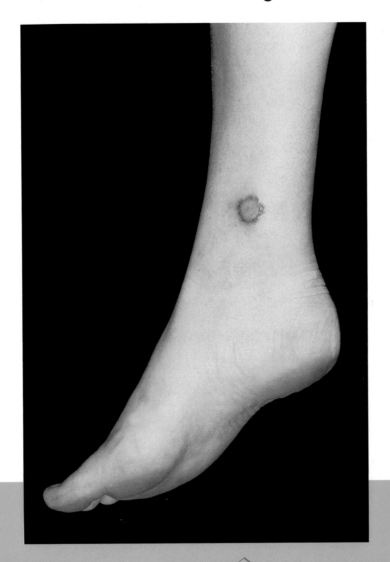

Thinking about Black Widow Spiders

Which of these black widow **spiders**
is the **male?** Which is the **female?**
How can you tell?

This female black widow has trapped a large **insect** in her **web.** She will use her **fangs** to bite it. What do her fangs put into the insect?

Black Widow Spider Map

(This is a female black widow spider.)

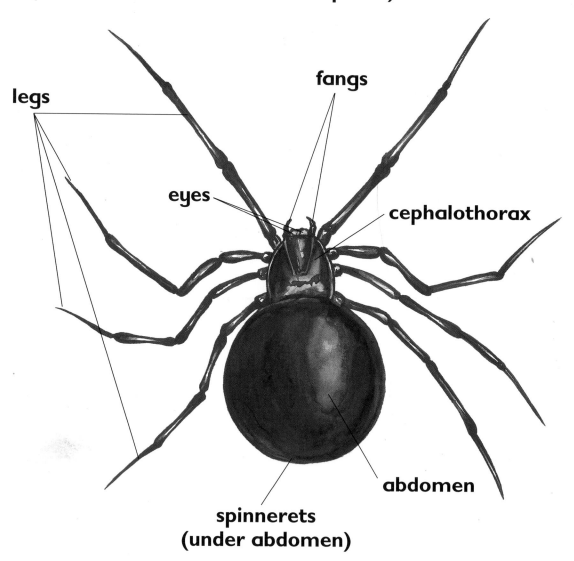

legs

fangs

eyes

cephalothorax

abdomen

spinnerets
(under abdomen)

Glossary

abdomen belly of an animal

adults grown-ups

arachnids group of animals that includes spiders, ticks, and scorpions

cannibalism when an animal eats one of its own kind

cephalothorax body part that has the head and chest together

egg sac silk bag that holds eggs

fang special mouthpart with a tube inside

female girl

hatch to come out of an egg

insect animal with six legs and three body parts

larvae young of an animal that looks like a worm

male boy

mate when a male and a female come together to make babies

molt get rid of skin that is too small

predator animal that hunts other animals for food

prey animal eaten by other animals

protect keep safe

silk thin, shiny thread

spider animal with eight legs that can make silk

spiderling baby spider

spinnerets body parts that makes silk

venom liquid that can harm an animal

venomous can harm an animal or make it very sick

web threads of silk put together to make a net

More Books to Read

Martin, Louise. *Black Widow Spiders*. Vero Beach, Fla.: The Rourke Book Company, Inc., 2002.

McGinty, Alice B. *The Black Widow Spider*. New York: Rosen, 2002.

Murray, Julie. *Black Widow Spiders*. Minneapolis: Abdo & Daughters, 2002.

Index